THE SILLIEST JOKE BOOK EVER!

With special thanks to the
patrons of Jeans for Genes 2003,
Brian Dowling and Amanda Holden.

PUFFIN BOOKS

Published by the Penguin Group
Penguin Books Ltd, 80 Strand, London WC2R ORL, England
Penguin Putnam Inc., 375 Hudson Street, New York, New York 10014, USA
Penguin Books Australia Ltd, 250 Camberwell Road, Camberwell, Victoria 3124, Australia
Penguin Books Canada Ltd, 10 Alcorn Avenue, Toronto, Ontario, Canada M4V 3B2
Penguin Books India (P) Ltd, 11 Community Centre, Panchsheel Park, New Delhi – 110 017, India
Penguin Books (NZ) Ltd, Cnr Rosedale and Airborne Roads, Albany, Auckland, New Zealand
Penguin Books (South Africa) (Pty) Ltd, 24 Sturdee Avenue, Rosebank 2196, South Africa

Penguin Books Ltd, Registered Offices: 80 Strand, London WC2R ORL, England

www.penguin.com

First published 2003
020

British Library Cataloguing in Publication Data
A CIP catalogue record for this book is available from the British Library

ISBN-13: 978-0-141-31576-8

www.greenpenguin.co.uk

ALWAYS LEARNING   **PEARSON**

The SiLLiEST JOKE BOOK EVER!

PUFFIN

WHAT IS JEANS FOR GENES?

Jeans for Genes raises funds for research into genetic disorders affecting children and provides valuable support services for families.

In the UK, one baby in every thirty-three is born with a genetic disorder or birth defect. That's one baby born every thirty minutes whose life is affected.

There are over 4,000 recognized genetic disorders, many of which are life-threatening and have no current cure.

Research carried out with Jeans for Genes proceeds is giving great hope to thousands of families across the nation.

For further information, call the Jeans for Genes freephone hotline 0800 980 4800 or visit **www.jeansforgenes.com**

EIGHT NATIONAL CHARITIES WORKING TOGETHER TO HELP SICK CHILDREN

The net proceeds of the 2003 Jeans for Genes Campaign™ received between 1st July 2003 and 30th June 2004 will be distributed among these eight charities.

Great Ormond Street Hospital Children's Charity
Reg. Charity No. 235825
©1989 GOSHCC

The Primary Immunodeficiency Association
Reg. Charity No. 803217

The Chronic Granulomatous Disorder Research Trust
Reg. Charity No. 1003425

The Society for Mucopolysaccharide Diseases
Reg. Charity No. 287034

The Jennifer Trust for Spinal Muscular Atrophy
Reg. Charity No. 327669

Rett Syndrome Association UK
Reg. Charity No. 327309

Batten Disease Family Association
Reg. Charity No. 1084908

The Haemophilia Society
Reg. Charity No. 288260

CONTENTS

WELCOME TO The SiLLiEST JOKE BOOK EVER,

where there are so many fantastic jokes, it is quite ridiculous. And you know these jokes must be funny, as you donated them through the Jeans for Genes joke competition! There were so many hilarious jokes, we had a difficult time trying to pick the winner. See the next page to find out if it was you!

So here they are – a riotous selection of the best jokes around. Don't forget to keep an eye out for our celebrities' favourite jokes – they are the silliest of the lot!

And best of all, by buying this book not only are you guaranteed great laughs, but you are helping the Jeans for Genes Campaign™ led by the Great Ormond Street Hospital Children's Charity.

WINNER

OF THE JEANS FOR GENES
JOKE COMPETITION

Once upon a time, there was
an inflatable boy who went to
an inflatable school and was taught
by an inflatable teacher.
One day, the boy brought a pin
to school. The teacher said,
'You've let the school down,
you've let me down, but most of all,
you've let yourself down!'

THOMAS LINDSAY

JOKES FOR JEANS

YOU JUST WON'T BE ABLE TO WEAR THESE GAGS!

Why did the scientist wear denim?
Because he was a jean-ius.

When can you see an elephant fly?
If you look in the front of an elephant's jeans.

Which superhero wears jeans?
Denim denim denim denim denim denim BATMAN!

Which are the world's saddest trousers?
Blue jeans.

What is made of denim and lives inside a lamp?
A jean-ie

Why did the lifeboat man throw his jeans in the air?
Someone told him to throw up flares.

What's blue and white and can't climb trees?
A fridge with a denim jacket on.

What's brown and blue
and swings through the jungle?
A monkey with a denim jacket on!

FAMILY FROLICS

HAVE A RIOT WITH THESE RIDICULOUS RELATIVES!

Did you hear about the little boy
who pushed his father into the fridge?
He wanted pop.

Sister: 'What shall I do? My teacher says
I've got to write an essay on a monster.'
**Brother: 'Well, first, you're going to need
a very big ladder ...'**

Grandad: 'I'd really like a job
I can get my teeth into.'
Grandma: 'Well, here's a glass of water.'

S CLUB 8

What's pink, small,
wrinkly and belongs
to Grandpa?
Grandma.

Did you hear about the very well-behaved
little boy? When he was good, his father
would give him 50p and a pat on the head.
By the time he was sixteen, he had
£1,000 and a very flat head.

One of James's chores was
to feed the cat after school.
'Have you seen the cat bowl?'
he asked his elder sister.
'No, is she any good?' she replied
absent-mindedly.

Sally had her friend Polly over to play.
Big brother Jack asked, 'Is that your real face
or are you wearing a mask?'
'I didn't come here to be insulted,'
Polly sniffed.
'Oh – well where do you usually go?'
Jack asked.

It was a big day in the Robinson household –
Andrew was leaving for boarding school.
'Here you are, son,' said his father as he
gave him a small parcel.
'Oh, a comb – um, thanks, Dad,' said Andrew.
'Just think of it as a parting gift,'
said his father.

One day, a father was putting his son to bed. He kissed him goodnight and went downstairs. A few minutes later, the son called out, 'Dad, can I have a glass of water?'

The father called up, 'No! Now go to sleep!'

A few minutes later he heard, 'Dad, can I have a glass of water?'

'No! Now go to sleep or I'll come up there!' he called out. Then he heard, 'Dad, when you come up here can you bring me a drink of water?'

After a visit to the circus, George and his elder brother were talking about the acts.

'I didn't think much of the knife-thrower, did you?' said George.

'I thought he was brilliant,' said his brother.

'Well, I didn't,' said George. 'He kept chucking those knives at that soppy girl, and he never hit her once ...'

What did the father bee say
after a hard day's work?
'Honey, I'm home!'

Aunty Pam to her small niece:
'I hear you have a new little brother.'
Lucy: 'Yes.'
Aunty Pam: 'And what's his name,
sweetheart?'
Lucy: 'I don't know. He won't tell me.'

'No, I can't possibly see you today,'
said the harassed mother to the
door-to-door salesman.
'That's great,' said the persistent
businessman. 'I'm selling spectacles!'

A little boy one day went up to his grandfather and said, 'Grandpa, can you make a noise like a frog?' His grandfather replied, 'Why's that, sonny?' and the little boy said, 'Cos Mum says when you croak it we are all going to Florida!'

Mum: 'Poor Jeremy, did the bee sting you?'
Jeremy (crying): 'Yes.'
Mum: 'I'll put some cream on it, then.'
Jeremy (stops crying):
'Don't be stupid, Mum.
It'll be miles away now!'

REALLY
SiLLY JOKES

HAVE A GIGGLE WITH THESE GROAN-MAKING GAGS.

What's yellow and green and
hangs from trees?
Giraffe snot.

What do you call a fairy
who has never had a bath?
Stinkerbell.

Who earns a living
driving their customers away?
A taxi driver.

What cheese is made backwards?
Edam.

HOLLY VALANCE

Where do you find a
tortoise with no legs?
Where you left it.

Who invented fire?
Some bright spark.

What is green and
as tall as a tree?
A bogey on stilts.

Why is it difficult to open a piano?
Because the keys are on the inside.

What do a criminal and a
pub landlord have in common?
They both spend a lot of time behind bars.

'Eat up your spinach,
it'll put colour in your cheeks.'
'But I don't want green cheeks!'

There were five cats on the edge of a cliff.
One jumped off. How many were left?
None. They were all copycats.

Why did the biscuit cry?
Because his mother had been a wafer so long.

Why did the farmer steamroll his field?
To grow mashed potatoes.

What do you call a man
with a shovel on his head?
Doug.

What do you call a man
with a seagull on his head?
Cliff.

What do you call a man
with a stamp on his head?
Frank.

JODIE KIDD

What do you call
a man standing in a
pile of leaves?
Russell.

What's the hardest part
about milking a gerbil?
Getting the bucket under it.

What did one virus say to another?
'Stay away! I think I've got penicillin!'

Why does a milking stool
only have three legs?
Because the cow has the udder.

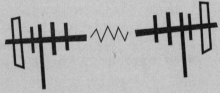

Two aerials meet on a roof, fall in love and
get married. The ceremony was rubbish
but the reception was fantastic.

What is a volcano?
A mountain with hiccups.

Did you hear about the man who
drowned in his breakfast muesli?
He was dragged in by a strong currant.

'Give me a sentence using the word
"indisposition".'
'I always play goalie because I like
playing in-disposition.'

A jump lead walks into a bar.
The barman says, 'I'll serve you,
but don't start anything ...'

What do you get if you cross
a werewolf with a flower?
I don't know, but I'm not going to
smell it to find out.

FAY RIPLEY

Why did the crab blush?
Because the sea weed ...

What did the sea say to the ocean?
Nothing, it just waved.

What kind of hair do oceans have?
Wavy.

What do angels say
when they answer the phone?
Halo.

What do you call a boomerang
that won't come back?
A stick.

What is the one question you can
never answer 'yes' to, truthfully?
'Are you asleep?'

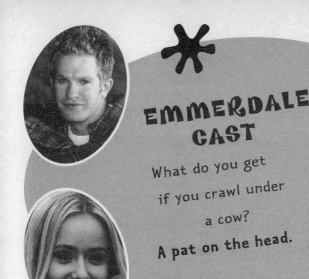

EMMERDALE CAST

What do you get
if you crawl under
a cow?
A pat on the head.

Why do eggs avoid telling jokes?
They crack each other up.

Why was the man fired
from the orange juice factory?
He just couldn't concentrate.

Who can jump higher
than a house?
Anyone. A house can't jump.

Why is the ocean friendly?
Because it always waves.

What do you call two robbers?
A pair of knickers.

'You must think I'm a perfect fool.'
'No, you aren't perfect ...'

What kind of beans can't you grow?
Jelly beans.

What runs around Paris at
lunchtime in a plastic bag?
The lunch-pack of Notre Dame.

20

What runs
around a field
but never moves?
A fence.

What goes ha ha ha, plop?
Someone laughing their head off.

What is brown and sticky?
A stick.

What did the Maths textbook say to
the other Maths textbook?
I'm tired of solving all your problems.

What is orange and sounds
like a parrot?
A carrot.

Why did the scarecrow
get a Nobel prize?
**Because he was
outstanding in his field.**

Have you heard the joke
about the garbage tip?
It's rubbish.

Why did the tomato blush?
**Because it saw the
salad dressing.**

What do you do if you see
a spaceman?
You park in it, man.

DAVID JASON

How do locomotives hear?

Through their engineers.

Two peanuts were walking down the road. **Unfortunately, one was a salted.**

What did the girl light bulb say to the boy light bulb? **'I love you watts and watts.'**

What do you call an
American drawing?
A Yankee doodle.

What did one invisible man
say to the other?
'It's nice not to see you again.'

What happened when the man walked
through a screen door?
He strained himself.

What is Beethoven
up to these days?
Decomposing.

ANIMAL ANTICS

JOKES TO BRING OUT THE **BEAST** IN YOU!

Mum: 'Julie, put some more water in the fish tank.'
Julie: 'But Mum, I only put some in yesterday and he hasn't finished drinking that yet!'

When should a mouse carry an umbrella?
When it's raining cats and dogs.

Where do tadpoles change?
In a croak-room!

SARA COX

Once there was a swimming race to cross the Channel, and two cats were taking part. There was an English cat, whose name was One, Two, Three – and a French cat whose name was Un, Deux, Trois ... The race began and both cats were neck and neck until all of a sudden, a huge wave washed over them. One, Two, Three was a strong swimmer and was the only one to reach the other side and win the race. Why?

Cos Un, Deux, Trois, Quatre, Cinq!

What do penguins use
for napkins?
Flap-kins.

Why did the pig go to the casino?
To get filthy rich.

How does a flea get around?
By itch-hiking.

What do you get if you cross
a kitten and a ball of wool?
Mittens.

How do you stop a polar bear
from charging?
Take away its credit card.

What type of sandals do frogs
like to wear?
Open-toed.

Why didn't the cow worry
when he lost his voice?
Because no moos is good news.

Keith: 'I haven't slept for days.'
Kate: 'Why not?'
Keith: 'I sleep at night.'

Why do giraffes have
such long necks?
**Cos their heads are so far away
from their bodies.**

What did the bird get
when he was sick?
Tweet-ment.

Why did the turkey
cross the road?
He was disguised as a chicken.

How does the family dog
contact his friends?
On the tele-bone.

STEPHEN GATELY

What do you get if you pour hot water down a rabbit hole?

Hot cross bunnies.

How does a cat who doesn't have any money describe itself?

Paw.

Did you hear about the dog who visited a flea circus?

He stole the show.

Why did the crab go to prison?
Because he kept on pinching people's bottoms.

What did
the mummy bee
say to the baby bee?
Beehive yourself.

Two fish are in a tank. One turns to the other and says, 'Hard to drive these things, isn't it?'

What happened when
the sheepdog ate too much jelly?
He got the collie-wobbles.

Why should you never
play games with skunks?
**Because if they catch you cheating
they kick up a stink.**

What goes dot-dot-dot,
dash-dash-dash, dot-dot?
A leopard in a hurry.

What do you call a bird with no eye?
A brd.

What do you call a bee who has had a spell put on him?
He's bee-witched.

What does a bee get in a chippy?
A hum-burger.

Why did the monkeys leave the circus?
They were tired of working for peanuts.

What snakes are good at sums?
Adders.

What do you
call a slug?
**A homeless
snail.**

What is a snail?
**A slug with a
crash helmet.**

How do snails get
their shiny shells?
Snail varnish.

What bird is always
out of breath?
A puffin.

!

What do you call a hamster
who can pick up a horse?
Sir.

What sound do hedgehogs
make when they kiss?
'Ouch.'

Why is a Dalmatian
no good at hide-and-seek?
**Because he is always
getting spotted.**

What must you do to save
a drowning mouse?
**Use mouse-to-mouse
resuscitation.**

What do you call a donkey with three legs?
A wonkey.

What do baby apes sleep in?
Apri-cots.

How do sheep keep warm?
Central bleat-ing.

What do you get if you
cross a cow with a millionaire?
Rich milk.

AMANDA
HOLDEN

Why do ducks
walk softly?
**Cos they can't
walk hardly!**

36.

Why do giraffes have such
long necks?
**Because they've got such
stinky feet.**

What do you do if you come
face-to-face with an adder?
Subtract it.

What's the best job for a spider?
A website builder.

How can you tell how old a snake is?
**If it has a rattle, it must
be a baby.**

What do you call a gorilla with
a couple of bananas in his ears?
**Anything you like –
he can't hear you!**

What do you get if you cross a
kangaroo with a sheep?
A woolly jumper.

What does a frog eat
with his burger?
French flies.

What's the definition
of a caterpillar?
A worm in a fur coat.

38

What do you call
singing insects?
Humbugs.

What is a grasshopper?
An insect on a pogo stick.

Why did the lizard go on a diet?
**Because it weighed too much
for its scales.**

How many skunks does it take
to make a big stink?
A phew.

What films do
penguins like best?
Black and white ones.

If a crocodile makes shoes,
what does a banana make?
Slippers.

What did the Scottish owl sing?
Owld Lang Syne.

Whats a frog's
favourite sweet?
A lolli-hop.

What is a frog's
favourite drink?
Croka-cola!

Where do you find a
dinosaur cow?
In a moo-seum.

What do you call a
one-eyed dinosaur?
Do-you-think-he-saw-us?

41

A mummy polar bear and a baby polar bear are at the North Pole sitting on their icebergs, when the baby polar bear says, 'Mummy, am I really a polar bear?' She replies, 'Of course you are, darling. Your dad is a polar bear, I am a polar bear and you are a polar bear.'

Ten minutes later the baby polar bear looks at his mum and says, 'Mummy, am I really, really a polar bear?' She replies, 'Of course you are, darling. Your dad is a polar bear, I am a polar bear and you are a polar bear.'

Ten minutes later the baby polar bear again looks at his mum and says, 'Mummy, am I really, really, really a polar bear?' She gets a little annoyed now and says, 'I have told you, of course you are a polar bear. Your dad is a polar bear and I am a polar bear. Why do you keep asking me?'

To which the baby polar bear replies, 'Because, Mum, I'm bloomin' freezing!'

ALISTAIR McGOWAN

in memory of his dad

Two policemen were driving down a little country lane when this chicken overtakes them doing 50 mph. The two policemen cannot believe what they have seen and decide to give chase. They follow the chicken for some time when suddenly it turns into a little farmyard. They search the area but cannot find it. The farmer comes out and asks them what they are doing. The two policemen tell him that a chicken overtook them at 50 mph and that they have come to find it.

'Oh, that'll be one of my three-legged chickens,' said the farmer. 'Why have you got three-legged chickens?' asked the policemen. 'Search me,' said the farmer. 'I haven't caught one!'

43

One day, a family of tortoises decided
to go for a picnic. So Mummy tortoise,
Daddy tortoise and Baby tortoise set off
with a picnic basket full of goodies.
First they had to cross a road, which
took them one day, then two days to
cross a river, then two days to cross a
field to get to the picnic area.

As Mummy tortoise was unpacking the
cake, she realized she had forgotten to
pack the cutlery. 'Oh no,' she said.
'We can't eat the cake, we have nothing
to cut it with!'

'Baby tortoise will have to go back
and get the knives and forks, while
Mummy and I guard the picnic,'
said Daddy tortoise.

'I will only go if you promise not to
eat any of the cake while I am gone.'
Mummy and Daddy both agreed and
so Baby set off.

Two days passed and Daddy said, 'Baby will be at the river now.' Another two days passed and Mummy said, 'Baby will be at the road now.' Another day passed and Daddy said, 'Baby will be at home now, getting the knives and forks.' Another three days passed and Mummy said, 'Baby would have crossed the road and the river by now, another two days to go and he will be here.' Two days passed and Baby had not arrived. Daddy said, 'He has probably been delayed along the way, not long now.' Another five days passed and Baby still had not returned, and so Mummy said, 'We had better eat this cake before it goes off.'

'Okay,' replied Daddy, and as they were about to eat their first mouthful, Baby appeared from behind a bush and said, 'Right, that's it, I'm not going to get the knives and forks now!'

CAROL VORDERMAN

What is worse than a
giraffe with a sore neck?
A centipede with corns.

What is a bear's favourite drink?
Koka-Koala!

Why did the spider buy a car?
So he could take it out for a spin.

What do cows do on a night out?
They go to the moo-vies.

What do you call a canary
that's been run over by a lawnmower?
Shredded tweet.

What does a spider do
when he gets angry?
He goes up the wall.

What do you get if you cross
a duck and some cream?
Cream quackers.

A man couldn't decide what pet to get so he
walked into a pet shop and bought a millipede
in a box. He took it home and tapped on the
box, and said, 'Would you like to come out
and play?' There wasn't any answer.
Two minutes later he tapped on the box and
said 'Would you like to come out and play?'
But there was no answer.

He waited five minutes and tapped on the
box again, and said 'Would you like to come
out and play?' Then he heard a voice say,
'Will you hold on a minute, I'm putting
my shoes on!'

47

'Do you have any
dogs going cheap?'
**'I'm afraid not.
They go woof, woof.'**

What do insects learn at school?
Moth-ematics.

What's the difference between
a fly and a bird?
A bird can fly but a fly can't bird.

What do you call a
fish with no eyes?
A fsh.

What do you call a
pig with three eyes?
Piiig.

Why didn't the lobster share?
Because he was shellfish.

What does a frog say in the library?
'Read it, read it, read it ...'

Why were the mum and dad owls
worried about their son?
**He didn't seem to give
a hoot any more.**

EVEN !
SiLLiER
JOKES

NOW, IF YOU THINK THE JOKES
IN THE LAST SECTION WERE STUPID, READ ON ...

A brown paper cowboy rode into town
on a brown paper horse wearing a brown paper
hat, brown paper trousers and a brown paper
jacket. Strapped to his waist was a brown
paper gun. The town sheriff shouted,
'I'm arresting you.'

'What for?' asked the brown paper cowboy.

'Rustling.'

What is black and white and made of wax?

A pandle.

What did the 0
say to the 8?
'Nice belt.'

What did the 1
say to the 11?
'I like your friend.'

TESS DALY

What do you call a
husband and wife
fishing together?
Rod and Annette.

How do you make an apple puff?
Chase it around the garden.

What does a tree drink?
Root beer!

What's white and goes up?
A silly snowflake.

Did you hear about the magic tractor?
**It went down the lane and
turned into a field.**

Why can't penguins fly?
**Because they are
chocolate biscuits.**

What do you get swinging from trees?
Sore arms.

What happened to the dog that
swallowed a firefly?
It barked with de-light.

What do you call a nervous celery stalk?
An edgy veggie.

CLAIRE GOOSE

What do
hippies do?
**Hold up your
leggies.**

53

What do snowmen eat for breakfast?

Snowflakes.

What did the big chimney
say to the little chimney?

'You're far too young to smoke.'

If buttercups are yellow,
what colour are hiccups?

Burp-le.

What runs but never walks?

Water.

Why did the tap dancer give up?
He kept falling in the sink.

Did you hear about the actor
who fell through the floor?
**It was just a stage he was
going through.**

What did the blizzard
say to the tornado?
'Shall we play draughts?'

Why did the rock star suddenly
feel cold at the concert hall?
**The place was crammed
with fans.**

What is the fastest cake in the world?
Too late, it's scone.

A man who worked at the grocer's shop
was six feet tall, had red hair and wore
size eleven shoes. What did he weigh?
Vegetables.

BRIAN DOWLING

What do you do
if you split your
sides laughing?
**Run till you get
a stitch.**

Luke Skywalker and his dad Darth Vader are sitting round the tree on Christmas morning. Luke goes to open his first present when Darth stops him and says, 'Wait, Luke, I know what that present is, it's a teddy bear.' Sure enough, Luke opens the present and it's a teddy bear. He goes to open his next present, but Darth again stops him and tells him it is a train set. Luke is amazed and starts to open his last present. Before he can get the paper off, Darth says, 'That's a new jumper, Luke.'

Luke is amazed by this and asks Darth how he knew what they all were.

Darth turns to him and says, 'I felt the presents, Luke ...'

What's black and white and red all over?
A newspaper!

What's black and white and red all over?
A bashful zebra!

A fried egg, a sausage and two rashers of bacon walk into a bar and ask for a drink. The barman refuses, saying, 'Sorry, we don't serve breakfast here.'

What is the difference between a grizzly bear and a biscuit?
You can't dip a grizzly in your cup of tea.

Why was six scared of seven?
Because seven, eight, nine.

CLAIRE SWEENEY

A lorry-load of tortoises crashed into a train-load of terrapins.
It was a turtle disaster.

CHICKEN CHUCKLES

ASK YOURSELF, DO YOU FEEL CLUCKY, KID?

Why don't
chickens like people?
They beat eggs.

Why did the chicken
cross the basketball court?
He heard the referee calling, 'Fowl!'

What happened to the young chicken
that misbehaved at school?
He was egg-spelled.

What do you get if you cross a chicken
with a cement mixer?
A brick-layer.

What did the
sick chicken say?
'I have the people pox.'

Why is it easy for chicks to talk?
Because talk is cheep.

What happens when a hen eats gunpowder?
She lays hand gren-eggs.

Why did the chicken cross the net?
It wanted to get to the other site.

What do you call a rooster who wakes you
up at the same time every morning?
An alarm cluck.

How do chickens
encourage their babies?
They egg them on.

Why did the chicken cross the road?
**Because the grass is always
greener on the other side.**

Why did the chewing gum cross the road?
**Because it was stuck to the
chicken's foot.**

Why did the one-eyed chicken
cross the road?
To get to the bird's eye shop.

JUMBO JAPES

HEARD THE ONE ABOUT THE ELEPHANT?

How do you know you have an
elephant hiding under your bed?
When your nose hits the ceiling.

How do you know when an
elephant has been in your fridge?
When there are footprints in the jelly.

What does an elephant
use to call his friends?
An ele-phone.

Why did the elephant paint her head yellow?
**To see if blondes really do
have more fun.**

What do you get if you cross a pigeon
with an elephant?
Lots of anxious pedestrians.

Why do elephants paint their feet yellow?
So they can hide upside down in the custard.

JULIE WALTERS

A mouse and an elephant met in a
clearing in a jungle, and the mouse said to the
elephant, 'Gordon Bennett, you are absolutely
enormous!' So the elephant replied,
'Gosh yeah, you're absolutely tiny.'
And the mouse said, 'Yes, but I haven't
been very well lately.'

63

What's the difference between
an elephant and an aspirin?
**If an elephant was small, white
and smooth, he'd be an aspirin.**

Have you ever seen an elephant
hiding upside down in the custard?
No? It must work then.

What do you get if you
cross an elephant with a flea?
Lots of worried-looking dogs.

What's the difference
between an elephant and a biscuit?
**You can't dunk an elephant
in your tea.**

What's the difference
between an elephant and a post box?
'You don't know? I'm not sending
you to post my letters then!'

A policeman stopped a man who was
walking along with an elephant and
ordered him to take it to the zoo
at once. The next day the policeman
saw the same man, still with the
elephant.
'I thought I told you to take that
elephant to the zoo,' he said.
'I did,' said the man, 'and now I'm
taking him shopping.'

How do you get four
elephants in a Mini?
Two in the front,
two in the back.

CLASSROOM CAPERS

IF ONLY SCHOOL WAS THIS MUCH FUN!

Billy came home from a school camping trip.
'Did your tent leak?' asked his father.
'Only when it rained,' replied Billy.

Fred: 'On our last school trip,
the school bus got a puncture.'
Joe: 'How did it happen?'
Fred: 'There was a fork in the road.'

A party of school children went for a
trip in the country and one of them found
a pile of empty milk bottles.
'Look, Miss, I've found a cow's nest.'

A teacher told his class that he wanted some responsible children to go to the museum. A girl replied, 'You can put me down, because every trip I go on something gets damaged and I'm always responsible.'

The class were on a nature trail, when Jimmy said to the teacher, 'What has eight legs, six eyes, pink spots and purple spikes down its back?' The teacher replied, 'I've never heard of such a thing.'
'Well,' said Jimmy, 'there's one on your back right now.'

'If there are any fools in the room, will they please stand up,' said the sarcastic teacher. After a long silence, one boy rose to his feet. 'Now then, why do you consider yourself to be a fool?' sneered the teacher. 'Well, actually I don't,' said the boy, 'but I hate to see you standing up there all by yourself!'

'Now, children,' said the teacher, 'there's a wonderful example for us in the life of the ant. Every day the ant goes to work. Every day the ant is busy. And in the end, what happens?'
A voice comes from the back of the room, 'Somebody steps on him.'

Teacher: 'Your homework seems to be in your father's handwriting.'
Sam: 'Yes, I used his pen.'

Headmaster: 'You missed school yesterday, didn't you, Lucy?'
Lucy: 'Yes, I know. I'll aim properly next time.'

Darren: 'My baby sister has been walking for three months now!'
Susan (yawning): 'Really? She must be quite tired by now.'

Teacher: 'Why are you so late?'

Jenny: 'Well, I was obeying that sign saying, "School ahead, go slow".'

Edward was a very religious boy. He would never do his homework if there was a Sunday in the week.

Where are teachers made?

On an assembly line.

Teacher: 'David, didn't you hear me call you?'

David: 'Yes, but you told me not to answer back.'

Teacher: 'Felicity, I hope I didn't see you copying from Angela's work.'

Felicity: 'I hope you didn't, too.'

School nurse: 'Have you ever had trouble with pneumonia?'

Louise: 'Only when I have tried to spell it!'

69

Nicole: 'Today my teacher yelled at me for something I didn't do.'

Dad: 'What was that?'

Nicole: 'My homework!'

Asked to write an essay on water, little Willie thought for a moment and then wrote, 'Water is a colourless liquid that turns dark when you wash it.'

Teacher: 'James, how do you spell chrysanthemum?'

James: 'Well, if you don't know, how am I supposed to?'

Biology teacher: 'Tell me something about the mint plant.'

Pupil: 'It makes money.'

Billy: 'I learnt today that words can be very hurtful.'

Mother: 'Has that nasty Tommy been teasing you again?'

Billy: 'No, I dropped a big heavy dictionary on my foot!'

A pupil was having his very first French lesson. He didn't understand a word that the teacher was saying. He put up his hand and asked,

'Could I please go to the toilet?'

'Oui oui,' answered the teacher.

'Not at all, just a drink of water.'

71

Teacher: 'Could you tell me something about Einstein's Theory of Relativity?'
Pupil: 'Well, there was Grandma and Grandad Einstein, Mr and Mrs Einstein and their son Albert ...'

The teacher said to the class,
'Write me a project on the
Tower of London.'
One small girl piped up,
'Please Miss, I'd rather write on paper!'

Teacher: 'What is the capital of France?'
Sarah: 'F, I expect.'

Teacher: 'What is the difference
between a German student and
an English student?'
Susie: 'Hundreds of miles.'

Why is homework always boring?
**Because it makes holes in
your free time.**

A man escaped from prison by digging
a hole from his cell to the outside
world. When he finally emerged he
found himself in the middle of
a preschool playground.
'I'm free, I'm free!'
he shouted.
**'So what?' said a little girl.
'I'm four!'**

SPORTING SHENANIGANS

A GOOD SPORT ISN'T HARD TO FIND!

What has twenty-two legs, eleven heads,
two wings and goes 'Crunch'?
A football team eating crisps.

Why did the liquorice go jogging?
Because it was a liquorice all-sport.

Where does a swimmer sit down to eat?
At a pool table.

Why was the centipede dropped
from the football team?
**Because he took too long to put his
boots on.**

What goes in pink and
comes out blue?
A swimmer in winter.

What did the owl say to
the football match?
There's a twit or two.

What does a goalie do
in his spare time?
He surfs the net.

Why can't cars play football?
They only have one boot.

Why is Cinderella no good at football?
**She keeps on running away
from the ball.**

What do bananas do best
in the gymnasium?
The splits.

What is the best way to win
a race against an athlete?
**Make sure they are wearing
run-resistant clothes.**

What does the winner lose
in a marathon?
His breath.

Why can't cows play football?
Because they have two left feet.

Why do fairy godmothers make
good football coaches?
**They always help you
get to the ball.**

Why do babies make the
best basketballers?
Because they are great dribblers.

What's the quietest game
in the world?
**Tenpin bowling –
because you can hear a pin drop.**

MONSTER MADNESS

THESE JOKES ARE SO BAD, THEY ARE FRIGHTENING!

What is worse than a
monster in a bad mood?
Nothing.

What is the best thing to do if
a monster breaks down your front door?
Run out the back door.

How do you raise a baby monster
that has been abandoned by its parents?
With a forklift truck.

PAULA RADCLIFFE

What do you get if you cross a sculptor and a werewolf?

Hairy Potter.

?

Why is Doctor Frankenstein such good fun?

Because he'll soon have you in stitches.

Why was Doctor Frankenstein never lonely?

He was good at making friends.

What is the best way to speak to a monster?

From a long distance.

Why are monsters' fingers
never more than eleven inches long?
Because if they were twelve inches
they would be a foot.

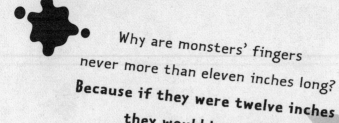

Father monster: 'Johnny,
stop making faces at that man.
How many times have I told you not to
play with your food?'

First Monster: 'That girl over there
just rolled her eyes at me.'
Second Monster: 'Don't you think
you had better roll them
back to her?'

What's big, green and smells?
A monster's bottom.

What's the difference
between a monster and a mouse?
**A monster makes bigger holes in
the skirting board.**

Did you hear about the monster
who went on a crash diet?
He wrecked three cars and a bus.

What do you get if you
cross a monster's brain with
an elastic band?
**A real stretch of
the imagination.**

?

What is a monster's
favourite ballet?
Swamp Lake.

What do you call a troll
who tries very hard?
An ogre-achiever.

On which day do monsters
eat people?
Chews-day.

What monster plays tricks on
Halloween?
Prank-enstein.

What happened to Ray the caveman
when he came face-to-face with a
Tyrannosaurus Rex?
He became an ex-Ray.

Why does a girl monster
kiss a boy monster on the
back of his neck?
Because that's where his lips are.

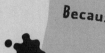

Why did the one-eyed monster
have to close down his school?
Because he only had one pupil.

What are prehistoric monsters
called when they sleep?
Dino-snores.

Where can you find giant snails?
At the end of giant's fingers.

GRUESOME GHOULS

THESE GHOSTS AND SKELETONS ARE QUITE A SCREAM!

What did the estate agent say to the ghost?
'I'm sorry, sir, but we have nothing suitable for haunting at the moment.'

What are a ghost's parents called?
Trans-parents.

How does an anxious ghost look?
Grave.

What is the best way for a ghost hunter to keep fit?
Exorcise regularly.

TAMZIN OUTHWAITE

Why didn't the skeleton want to play the piano?

His heart wasn't in it.

When do ghosts haunt skyscrapers?
When they are in high spirits.

What is the difference between a musician and a corpse?
One composes, the other decomposes.

Why are cemeteries such noisy places?
Because of all the coffin'.

What's a ghost's favourite
party game?
Hide-and-shriek.

What's a skeleton?
**Bones, with the people
scraped off.**

What skeleton was once
the Emperor of France?
Napoleon Bone-apart.

Did you hear about the stupid ghost?
He climbed over walls.

What kind of plate does
a skeleton eat off?
Bone china.

Why did the skeleton
go to the party?
**To have a rattling
good time!**

LORRAINE KELLY

Why didn't the skeleton
go to the disco?
**Because he had
'no body' to go with!**

What did one skeleton
prisoner say to another?
**If we had the guts,
we'd get out of here.**

What do you get if you
leave bones out in the sun?
A skele-tan.

Why did the one-handed
skeleton cross the road?
**To get to the
second-hand shop!**

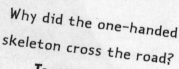

Why did the skeleton
go to the Chinese takeaway?
To get some spare ribs.

WICKED WITCHES AND VAMPISH VAMPIRES

THESE DASTARDLY DEVILS ARE REALLY QUITE A JOLLY LOT!

What's the most common
name for a witch?
Wanda.

Why do witches
always do well at English?
Because they are great spellers.

GARY LINEKER

Why did the wizard stop
telling fortunes?
He couldn't see any
future in it.

Did you hear about the wizard who
changed himself into an oil well?
He was really boring.

What's the difference between a
witch and the letters M, A, K, E, S?
**One makes spells and the other
spells makes.**

Why do wizards change
people into toads?
**Because if they changed them
into gorillas, they might
thump them.**

What do you call a witch's motorbike?
A barooom stick.

How do you make a witch itch?
Take away her 'w'.

What do you call a nervous witch?
A twitch.

What do you get
if you cross a witch with a pig?
A wart-hog.

What goes moorb moorb?
**A witch flying really
fast backwards.**

What do dragons wear?
Blazers.

Which creature is most likely
to have indigestion?
A goblin.

Why aren't pixies afraid of
witches and wizards?
**They have done an
elf-defence course.**

What does a witch hang
on her washing line?
Her abracada-bras.

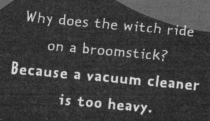

Why does the witch ride
on a broomstick?
**Because a vacuum cleaner
is too heavy.**

What is a vampire's
favourite dance?
The vaults.

What is a vampire's second
favourite dance?
The fang-dango.

What is a vampire's
favourite fruit?
Neck-tarines.

What is a vampire's favourite game?
Cricket – they never run out of bats.

What does a vampire take
for a bad cold?
Coffin drops.

What only goes out at night and goes
'Chomp, suck ... ouch!'?
A vampire with a rotten fang.

What did the barman say when the
ghost ordered a gin and tonic?
'Sorry, we don't serve spirits.'

What football team do vampires support?
Fang-chester United.

A vampire bat came home
one night with blood all over him.
His bat friends said, 'Ooh, where have
you been feasting tonight?' The bat told the
group of other bats to follow him,
so off the bats flew until they came
to a tree in the middle of the forest.
The bat then explained, 'You see
that tree? Well, I didn't!'

What do you call two crazy vampires?
Bats.

MEDICAL MARVELS

SCARED OF A VISIT TO THE DOCTOR? YOU WILL BE AFTER THESE JOKES!

'I keep on seeing big purple dots
in front of my eyes!'
'Have you seen a doctor?'
'No – just big purple dots!'

'Doctor, Doctor, I keep thinking I'm a spider!'
'What a web of lies!'

'Doctor, Doctor, can you help me out?'
**'Of course – just go through
that door and turn left.'**

'Doctor, Doctor, I keep thinking I'm a wigwam and a tepee!'
'**Calm down, you're two tents!**'

'Doctor, Doctor, I keep thinking I'm a moth!'
'**Get out of the way – you're in my light!**'

'Doctor, Doctor, my right leg really hurts.'
'**Don't worry about that, I expect that is just growing pains.**'
'But my left leg is growing just as fast, and that doesn't hurt a bit!'

'Doctor, Doctor, my hair keeps falling out!
Can't you give me something to keep it in?'
'**Certainly – how about this paper bag?**'

'Doctor, Doctor, I think I'm a witch!'
'You had better lie down for a spell.'

'Doctor, Doctor, I keep seeing sheep everywhere!'
'Have you seen anyone?'
'No, just sheep!'

'Doctor, Doctor, I keep thinking I'm a dog.'
'How long have you thought this?'
'Since I was a puppy.'

'Doctor, Doctor, my son has just
swallowed my pen. What should I do?'
'Use a pencil till I get there.'

'Doctor, Doctor, I've got a lettuce stuck in my mouth – and that's just the tip of the iceberg!

'Doctor, Doctor, I've only got fifty-nine seconds to live!'
'**Wait a minute, won't you?**'

'**Doctor, Doctor, I think I'm a bridge!**'
'What's come over you, man?'
'**Three lorries, seven cars and a bus!**'

'**Doctor, Doctor, I think I'm a dog!**'
'Take a seat.'
'**I can't, I'm not allowed on the furniture.**'

What is the best time to visit the dentist?
Tooth-hurty.

INCREDIBLY STUPID JOKES

GROAN AWAY,
AS THESE ARE THE WORST OF THE LOT!

How do you make a bandstand?
Take away the chairs.

What always ends everything?
The letter 'g'.

MARTIN KEMP

What did the window
say to the door?
'What are you squeaking
about – I'm the one
with the pane!'

Which side does a
duck have the most feathers?
The outside.

What do you call a
kernel of corn's father?
Popcorn.

What do you call a short man
with psychic abilities who has escaped
from prison?
A small medium at large.

'I just flew in from New York.'
'Wow! I bet your arms are tired!'

Why do birds fly south for the winter?
**Because they can't afford
to take a plane.**

Did you hear about the man who stole a truck
filled with rhubarb?
He was put into custard-y.

Alex: 'I snore so loudly I wake myself up.'
Alan: 'Try sleeping in the next room then.'

Customer: 'Waiter, waiter,
there isn't any chicken in my chicken pie!'
**Waiter: 'Well, you would hardly expect a
dog in a dog biscuit, would you?'**

What is rhubarb?
Celery in a rage.

What do you get when 5,000 strawberries
try to go through a door at once?
Strawberry jam.

TERRY WOGAN

What do you call a
pussycat that has
eaten a duck?
**A duck-filled
fatty puss.**

What's the best thing
to put in a Sunday roast?
Your teeth!

'Waiter, waiter, will my
sandwich be long?'
**'No madam, just the usual
square shape.'**

What's a Lap Lander?
**A clumsy person trying to
get off a bus.**

What is grey and has four legs
and a trunk?
A mouse going on holiday.

Two cannibals were eating a clown.
One says to the other, 'Is it just me or
does this taste funny to you?'

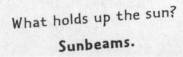

What holds up the sun?
Sunbeams.

Why did the boy take a
ruler to bed with him?
He wanted to see how long he slept.

Why did the boy take a pencil
to bed with him?
He wanted to draw the curtains.

What did the envelope say
to the stamp?
'Stick with me and we'll go places.'

Hamish: 'Do you always snore?'
Dougal: 'Only when I'm asleep.'

'Can you name ten animals starting with the letter P?'
'Sure – six parrots and four panthers!'

What did the pencil say to the pencil sharpener?
'Stop going in circles and get to the point.'

'My dog isn't very well. Do you know a good animal doctor?'
'I'm afraid I don't. All the doctors I know are people.'

What do you call a cow with no feet?
Ground beef.

What do you get if you cross
a parrot with a centipede?
A walkie-talkie.

What grows bigger
the more you take away?
A hole.

Why did the baker
work such long hours?
Because he kneaded the dough.

Why is it important not to play
chess with jungle animals?
**Because there are always
cheetahs about.**

I went to the butcher's the other day and I bet him £100 he couldn't reach the meat on the top shelf. And he said, 'No, I couldn't possibly – the steaks are too high.'

What's yellow and spins round and round?
A banana in a washing machine.

How do you make jam roly-poly?
Push it off the table.

What kind of shoes do bananas make?
Slippers.

What is a twip?
A twip is what a wabbit takes
when he wides a twain.

I went to buy some camouflage
trousers the other day but I
couldn't find any.

Two hydrogen atoms were out for a
walk in the park. 'Oh dear, I think
I have lost an electron,'
says the first one.
'Are you sure?' says the other.
'Oh yes,' replies the first,
'I'm positive.'

'Waiter, do you have frog's legs?'
'No, sir, I just walk this way.'

What do you get when you cross
a parrot with a shark?
A bird that will talk your ear off.

When is a door not a door?
When it's a-jar.

CAROLINE
QUENTIN
Why are there so many
Smiths in the phone book?
Because they
all have phones.

What is as big as Big Ben but
weighs nothing at all?
Big Ben's shadow.

Tim: 'My girlfriend is a peach.'
Ben: 'That's nice.'
Tim: 'No, it isn't. She has a heart of stone.'

I wish somebody would cross a chicken
with an octopus. That way, on Sundays,
everyone could have a leg.

What's the loudest dinner in the world?
Bangers and mash.

'Did you hear the joke
about the ocean?'
**'Don't worry – it'll be too deep
for me!'**

What do you call a nun with a
washing machine on her head?
Sister-matic.

A man spies a nice-looking lady in a
coffee shop. 'May I join you?' he asks.
**Alarmed, she asks,
'Why, am I coming apart?'**

What do you get when you
cross the bad girl of Brit Art with
the bad boy of rap?
Tracey Eminem

KNOCK, KNOCK

WHO DOESN'T HAVE A FAVOURITE KNOCK, KNOCK JOKE?

'Knock, knock.'
'Who's there?'
'Lucretia.'
'Lucretia who?'
'Lucretia from the Black Lagoon.'

'Knock, knock.'
'Who's there?'
'Elise.'
'Elise who?'
'Elise you don't have to tidy your room!'

'Knock, knock.'
'Who's there?'
'Juicy.'
'Juicy who?'
'Juicy my brand new dress?'

'Knock, knock.'
'Who's there?'
'Howl.'
'Howl who?'
'Howl I know unless you open the door?'

'Knock, knock'
'Who's there?'
'Luke.'
'Luke who?'
'Luke through the keyhole and you will find out!'

'Knock, knock.'
'Who's there?'
'Avenue.'
'Avenue who?'
'Avenue learnt my name yet?'

'Knock, knock.'
'Who's there?'
'Doctor.'
'Doctor who?'
'How did you guess?'

'Knock, knock.'
'Who's there?'
'Turner.'
'Turner who?'
'Turn around – there's a monster behind you!'

'Knock, knock.'
'Who's there?'
'Cows.'
'Cows who?'
'No, cows moo.'

'Knock, knock.'
'Who's there?'
'Granny.'
'Granny who?'

'Knock, knock.'
'Who's there?'
'Granny.'
'Granny who?'

'Knock, knock.'
'Who's there?'
'Lena.'
'Lena who?'
'Lean a little closer
and I'll tell you.'

'Knock, knock.'
'Who's there?'
'Granny.'
'Granny who?'

'Knock, knock.'
'Who's there?'
'Aunt.'
'Aunt who?'
'Aren't you glad
Granny's gone?'

'Knock, knock.'
'Who's there?'
'Boo.'
'Boo who?'
'Boo hoo – let me in! I've lost my key.'

'Knock, knock.'
'Who's there?'
'Ewan.'
'Ewan who?'
'No one else, just me!'

'Knock, knock.'
'Who's there?'
'Lemmie.'
'Lemmie who?'
'Lemmie alone,
can't you see I'm busy?'

'Knock, knock.'
'Who's there?'
'Ida.'
'Ida who?'
'Ida open the door,
if I were you!'

'Knock, knock.'
'Who's there?'
'Yolanda.'
'Yolanda who?'
'Yolanda me your pillow,
mine's fallen off the bed.'

'Knock, knock.'
'Who's there?'
'Gladys.'
'Gladys who?'
'Gladys you!'

119

'Knock, knock.'
'Who's there?'
'Jo.'
'Jo who?'
'Jo King!'

'Knock, knock.'
'Who's there?'
'Justin.'
'Justin who?'
'Just in time to
start thinking of
ideas for next year's
Jeans for Genes
day!'

CONTRIBUTORS

Puffin and the Jeans for Genes Day organizers would like to thank the following contributors:

Abi Bradshaw

Alex Duke

Alice Wood

Amy Bobin

Amy-Louise
O'Donnell

Andrew Ruff

Anneka Rutter

Ben Hickey

Bryn Eyles

Bryony Curtis

Carly Hings

Ceri Vaughan

Cheri-Anne Boxall

Chris Burgess

Chris Smith

Chris Sythes

Claire Dwyer

Danni Russell

Debbie Rhule

Dobby Cherkovsky

Elizabeth
Scott-Baumann

Elizabeth Woolner

Ella Preston

Emma Browse

Emma Yeates

Gemma Bradshaw
Gemma Haywood
Graeme Maclennan
Hannah Grantham
Hannah Picking
Heather McDonald
Helen Eaton
Isobel Belton
Jacqui McDonough
Jade Taylor
Jane Lawson
Jerry Brind
Joanna Baker
Jodie Walker
Joe Conneally
Joe Darbyshire
John Dyson

Karen Rudder
Kathryn Hatch
Katie John
Kelly Ward
Kimberly Lock
Kirsty Marchant
Kirsty Young
Laura Leigh
Lauren Proctor
Leanne Boddy
Lewis Mitcham
Lisa Stacey
Liz Dobbins
Lorna McDermid
Louise Tinsley
Lucy Claxton
Maria Kerr
Mary Atkinson

Matthew Priestley

Matthew Russell

Michaela Purvis

Nadia Mehnaaz

Nadine Coleman

Nancy Burgess

Naomi Norris

Naomi Vasey

Natalie Hill

Neil Walker

Nicola Woodley

Perry King

Rachael Russell

Rhys Eyles

Richard Allison

Rob Cowell

Robbie Spurgeon

Ros Saunders

Roxanne Sutton

Sarah Morris

Sarah Patten

Seamus Devlin

Senay Ashfield

Sharon Wegener

Shelley Baker

Simon Edwards

Sophie Leonard

Steven Marking

Stuart Allen

Tammy Webster

Thomas Clayton

Thomas Cullimore

Toni Koppelow

Tracy Eaton

Valentina Rice

Victoria Prince

Wayne Howard

THIS IS
THE END OF

!
?
GOODBYE!